ULTIMATE **MILITARY** MACHINES

HELICOPTERS

Tim Cooke

WAYLAND
www.waylandbooks.co.uk

WAYLAND

www.waylandbooks.co.uk

First published in Great Britain in 2015 by Wayland

Copyright © 2014 Brown Bear Books Ltd.

Wayland
An imprint of Hachette Children's Group
Part of Hodder & Stoughton
Carmelite House
50 Victoria Embankment
London EC4Y 0DZ
An Hachette UK Company
www.hachette.co.uk
www.hachettechildrens.co.uk

All Rights Reserved.

Dewey Number: 623.7'46'047-dc23
ISBN: 978 0 7502 9673 1
10 9 8 7 6 5 4 3 2 1

Brown Bear Books Ltd.
First Floor
9–17 St. Albans Place
London
N1 0NX

Managing Editor: Tim Cooke
Picture Manager: Sophie Mortimer
Art Director: Jeni Child
Editorial Director: Lindsey Lowe
Children's Publisher: Anne O'Daly
Production Consultant: Alastair Gourlay

Printed in China

CONTENTS

INTRODUCTION

Skimming the trees to land an assault force in enemy territory or to rescue the wounded, the helicopter is an essential military workhorse. The whir of rotor blades is the soundtrack of modern warfare. But only 50 years ago, the helicopter was unknown on the battlefeld.

HH-60G

Probe for mid-air refuelling

Anti-torque tail rotor

Winchman controls wire

SPECIFICATIONS
Max. load: 9,900 kg (22,000 lb)
Crew: 4
Blades: 4 front, 4 tail
Armament: 2 machine guns

PAVE HAWK

The Hawk uses night goggles and infrared systems for search-and-recovery missions in hostile environments.

4

AN AGE-OLD DREAM

For centuries, inventors imagined using spinning blades to power an aircraft. Italian artist Leonardo da Vinci designed a version of a helicopter over 500 years ago. But it was not until the 1920s that the first rotorcraft lifted into the air.

◀ Leonardo Da Vinci invented his corkscrew craft in the 1490s, but it was never built.

● SIKORSKY R-4

WORLD WAR II

The Sikorsky R-4 was the only mass-produced military 'chopper' of World War II (1939–1945).

THE KOREAN WAR

The Korean War (1950–1953) saw the first real use of helicopters in a war zone. They were mainly used to transport supplies and wounded soldiers.

A Sikorsky hovers above the ▲ ground in Korea while U.S. Marines load weapons into its cargo net.

ROTORCRAFT: A flying machine powered by a spinning blade or rotor.

WHAT IS A HELICOPTER?

A helicopter is any aircraft that takes off and lands vertically by using rotor blades to lift the craft into the air. Because helicopters can get to remote areas without the need for landing strips, they are far more flexible than ordinary aeroplanes.

CONVOY

DEFENCE

Helicopters are great combat machines. They fly low and hug the contours of the land. Their quiet engines and electronic defences help protect them.

▲ A line of Pave Hawk helicopters flies low on a mission. Helicopters often fly in groups so that they can protect one another from attack.

CONTOURS: The way a landscape rises and falls.

UH-1 HUEY

◀ Troops abseil down ropes while a UH-1 Huey hovers.

DELIVERY

One of the helicopter's key roles is to get troops or supplies into or out of the battle zone. Using helicopters means that forces do not have to rely on dangerous routes over land.

AH-64 APACHE

Four blades

30 mm M230 chain gun

STRIKE WEAPON

Some helicopters carry machine guns and bombs. The U.S. 101st Airborne Division used Apaches and Black Hawks to attack the Iraqi capital, Baghdad, in January 1991.

▲ The AH-64 Apache attack helicopter is used to lead combat missions.

ABSEIL: Term for quickly climbing down a rope.

HELICOPTER MISSIONS

Helicopters have many different roles. They carry personnel and supplies; they gather information; they destroy enemy tanks or submarines. But it is their ability to go anywhere that makes them so valuable to the military.

BELL UH-1 HUEY

Twin blades and a single engine

◀ The Huey is the world's most widely used helicopter. It first flew in 1956 and played a key role during the Vietnam conflict (1964–1973).

RESCUE

A Sikorsky H-5 picks up wounded U.S. Marines in Vietnam. Helicopters are vital to transport wounded soldiers to field hospitals.

FIELD HOSPITAL: A temporary hospital set up behind the front line.

AH-1 COBRA

STRIKE FORCE

Armed with tube-launched missiles, Cobras target enemy tanks and armoured fighting vehicles. They destroyed more than 200 Iraqi tanks during Operation Desert Storm.

SPECIFICATIONS

Max. load: 4,500 kg (10,000 lb)
Crew: 2
Blades: 2 main, 2 tail
Main armament: 4 or 8 guided missiles

SPECIAL OPS

Helicopters are ideal for covert operations. They are the best way to get special forces behind enemy lines without being discovered. Helicopters can also rescue military personnel if a mission goes wrong.

COVERT: Carried out in secret.

AT SEA

Helicopters are especially useful at sea. Needing little space, they can take off from and land on ships. They can hover for long periods, so they are ideal for search-and-rescue missions.

MAKING WAVES

An anti-submarine warfare (ASW) MH-60R Seahawk lowers a sonar buoy. If the buoy finds an enemy submarine, the chopper can attack with mines and depth charges.

▲ An SH-3 Sea King stands by on an aircraft carrier ready to rescue pilots from the sea.

COAST GUARD

Helicopters such as this HH-60 Jayhawk are vital to the U.S. Coast Guard. They are used for rescue and to patrol the long coastlines of the United States.

SONAR BUOY: A device that detects underwater sounds.

HEAVY DUTY

Transporter helicopters use twin rotors to lift heavy loads into a war zone. They can carry combat squads, artillery or even tanks. Whatever the load, the helicopter can take it up to the front line.

HEAVYWEIGHT

The Chinook helicopter has been vital to the military campaigns in Vietnam, Iraq and Afghanistan. It carried heavy loads and supplies to remote battlefields.

CH-47 CHINOOK

Cargo hooks can carry artillery pieces

Wide loading ramp at rear

SUPPLY DROP

TRANSPORTER

The Chinook uses its rear ramp to drop cargo or personnel by parachute. The Chinook's cargo hold can carry 8,845 kg (19,500 lb) of gear or up to 33 troops in full combat kit.

Reinforced packing for air drop

HELICOPTER FIREPOWER

Military helicopters can carry different levels of weaponry.
Some are not armed, while others carry machine guns.
A navy helicopter carries anti-submarine and anti-ship missiles.
An army gunship combines machine guns with missiles and
rockets to support ground troops.

GUNSHIP

The Russian Mi-24 Hind is a fast
gunship and attack helicopter. It
carries a combination of machine
guns, missiles, rockets and grenades.

"[That] helicopters are
eagerly sought in large
numbers by air forces
... all over the world
serves to underscore
their value."
BILL GUNSTON, RAF
PILOT & INSTRUCTOR

MI-24 HIND

'Double bubble' cockpit
for pilot and gunner

Stub wings carry
weapons

GUNSHIP: A helicopter that carries a powerful range of weapons.

EUROCOPTER TIGER

▲ The Eurocopter Tiger came into service in 2003. It is made from composite materials that can withstand cannon fire.

MULTITASKERS

Eurocopter Tigers are employed as strike aircraft, but are also used for reconnaissance. Unlike other helicopters, the pilot sits in the front and the gunner sits in the back. Eurocopters served in Afghanistan and Libya in 2011.

HEAVILY ARMED

The AH-1W Super Cobra carries four missiles on each wing. Its weapon power has made the Cobra a popular choice for the U.S. military since the Vietnam War.

Four missiles carried beneath stub wing

Rocket launcher

▶ Engineers on a U.S. warship inspect the missiles on an AH-1W Super Cobra before a mission.

COMPOSITE: A strong material formed by combining other materials.

ROCKETS AND MISSILES

Helicopters fire missiles at aerial and ground targets. Rockets are a type of missile with their own engines. In the 1940s, the U.S. Navy developed folding-fin aerial rockets (FFARs) to launch from aircraft.

HYDRA FFARS

SON OF MOUSE

The Hydra 70 is a modern form of the original FFAR, 'Mighty Mouse'. The folding fins make the rockets easier to carry. When the rocket is fired, the fins fold out. They keep the rocket stable in the air.

Wire-guided missiles are steered by thin wires attached to the helicopter. The wire uncoils as the missile flies towards its target.

SS-11

▶ The SS-11 wire-guided anti-tank missile was used until the late 1980s.

PROPELLANT: Fuel that powers an engine to create motion.

HAWK FAMILY

The Sikorsky Black Hawk UH-60 is highly flexible. Because it is easy to manoeuvre, it can be used in a range of combat roles. As well as carrying different types of weapons, it is used as a troop and cargo transporter.

"The Black Hawks ... were what kept the mobs at a distance."
MARK BOWDEN
UN REPRESENTATIVE,
SOMALIA, 1993

▶ The Black Hawk's storage pods carry extra fuel and weapons for long-range military operations.

BLACK HAWK

MH-60 SEAHAWK

Based on the UH-60 Black Hawk, the MH-60 Seahawk is used on aircraft carriers for search and rescue at sea and in combat. With its hinged tail, it does not take up too much room on board.

SEAHAWK

STORAGE POD: A hard-shelled case carried on a helicopter's wing.

HELICOPTER CREW

A helicopter carries various crew members. Pilots undergo specialist training and need many skills, including good co-ordination. Some helicopters carry gunners or weapons specialists; others carry a winchman who can be lowered to the ground on a strong cable.

SKILLED PILOTS

Helicopters are difficult to fly. The pilot has to make constant adjustments in order to keep the aircraft steady in bad weather or when under attack. The job needs high powers of concentration.

"The ability of the helicopter to hover and move in any direction ... gives a thrill."
JOHN FAY, WESTLAND TEST PILOT

CO-ORDINATION: The ability to make different movements at once.

● UH-60 BLACK HAWK

▲ A UH-60 Black Hawk lowers a winchman. At times like this, a helicopter is an easy target. The crew must get the job done fast.

WINCHMAN

Winchmen make rescues when a helicopter cannot land, such as over water or in mountains. The winch can lift an injured person in a special stretcher.

CONTROL

Helicopter missions are run by air traffic controllers. They use radar to help avoid mid-air collisions or to direct helicopter landings and take-offs on board aircraft carriers.

WINCH: A mechanical drum that winds and unwinds a rope or cable.

A CHANGING ROLE

Helicopter crews constantly have to adapt to changes in enemy tactics. The manoeuvrability of helicopters allows crews to change tactics fast.

CH-53D

AERIAL TRICKS

One attacking tactic is for a group of helicopters to approach a target in formation. Lined up at intervals, they can then direct constant gunfire from both sides of the column.

FLYING IN PAIRS

Solo helicopters can be quite vulnerable to enemy fire. As a defence against this, helicopters often fly missions in pairs. One 'chopper' leads the way, while the other provides fire cover.

▲ The Sea Stallions are the U.S. Marines' heavy lifters. They have machine guns on both sides.

FIRE COVER: Firing at the enemy to prevent it firing at another target.

UP AND DOWN

A helicopter is much more manoeuvrable than a fixed-wing aeroplane. It has VTOL (vertical take-off and landing), so it can get to remote sites. It can hover in one place. It can even go backwards. Pilots learn to manoeuvre quickly, tipping the helicopter this way and that.

▲ A French Super Puma turns steeply to avoid enemy fire.

AH-64 APACHE

SPECIFICATIONS
Max. load: 10,433 kg (23,000 lb)
Crew: 2
Blades: 4 front, 4 tail
Armament: Hellfire missiles

PEEK-A-BOO

The AH-64 Apache catches the enemy unawares. Flying low, it stays hidden by hills, forests or buildings before it leaves cover to fire its anti-tank missiles. It is ideal for armed reconnaissance.

HELICOPTER HISTORY

The combat role of helicopters has changed. First used in the Korean War (1950–1953), they were mainly deployed to evacuate wounded soldiers from the battlefield. Today, they are often used in the hunt for terrorists in inaccessible mountain regions.

KOREAN WAR

In the Korean War (1950–1953), combat often took place a long way from medical help. Helicopters took the wounded to Mobile Army Surgical Hospitals (MASH). Rapid evacuation saved many lives.

◀ An injured U.S. infantryman is lifted onto a helicopter that will transport him quickly to a hospital during the Korean War.

▼ A casevac helicopter took casualties to a MASH, which had life-saving equipment and trained medical personnel.

CASEVAC: A military term for 'casualty evacuation'.

VIETNAM

The use of helicopters changed dramatically in the Vietnam War (1964–1973). Vietnam's mountainous jungles were better suited to helicopters than aeroplanes. The U.S. Army used its helicopters to transport goods and troops, as well as to carry out attack missions.

▶ A wounded U.S. soldier is carried from the UH-1 Huey that has just evacuated him from the battle zone.

● HUEY HELP

● UH-1

◀ Hueys carried combat troops on missions in Vietnam. Helicopters were useful where there were no roads.

RESCUE

Helicopter search-and-rescue missions have saved many civilians as well as soldiers. The U.S. Coast Guard, U.S. Air National Guard and local rescue teams are kept busy rescuing people from anywhere they get into trouble.

"If a man is in need of rescue ... a direct lift aircraft could come in and save his life."
IGOR SIKORSKY

PLUCKED FROM THE SEA

A helicopter from the USS *Kearsarge* hoists a seriously ill man from a ship in the Caribbean Sea in 2008. The helicopter answered a distress call from the Norwegian vessel.

HH-60 PAVE HAWK

ON THE WAY

A winchman from a U.S. Air National Guard HH-60 Pave Hawk climbs down a rope ladder to rescue a swimmer from rough water beneath the Golden Gate Bridge in San Francisco.

EVACUATION: Moving someone from danger to safety.

BOSNIA

Since the end of World War II, the helicopter has been called into service across the globe. Peacekeeping forces now operate worldwide. During the 1990s, U.S. military personnel served in Bosnia in Europe. Since then, they have been engaged in Afghanistan and the Middle East.

SAVING SCOTT

In June 1995, U.S. Air Force pilot Scott O'Grady was shot down over hostile territory in Bosnia. Marine CH-53 helicopters from USS *Kearsarge* were deployed to find him. It took a week to locate and rescue Captain O'Grady.

▲ A Sea Stallion lands on USS *Kearsarge* during Operation Enduring Freedom, the U.S.-led fight against global terrorism.

"When in desperate need of evacuation, the approach of a rescue helicopter breaks down all cultural or language barriers."
MICHAEL HAMPSON, HELICOPTER EXPERT

DEPLOYED: Personnel who have been sent out for a particular task.

23

MODERN WARFARE

Helicopters play a key role in the United Nations (UN) peacekeeping forces that operate worldwide. The UN has responded to attacks from terrorists and militia groups in Africa, Europe, the Middle East and Asia.

BLACK HAWK DOWN

In 1993, elite U.S. soldiers went to Somalia in Africa to capture the warlord who had taken control of the capital, Mogadishu. Two Black Hawks were shot down. U.S. special forces fought to rescue their trapped colleagues, but there were many casualties.

"We got a Black Hawk going down. We got a Black Hawk going down. We got a Black Hawk crashed in the city."
U.S. RADIO TRAFFIC
MOGADISHU, 3 OCTOBER 1993

MILITIA: An irregular fighting unit formed by armed civilians.

DESTROYED

This is the wreckage of a Black Hawk helicopter on the ground in Somalia. It was shot down during the Battle of Mogadishu on 3–4 October 1993.

ENDURING FREEDOM

From 2001 to 2014, forces representing the UN were active in Afghanistan as part of Operation Enduring Freedom. Helicopters were used to carry troops and supplies to forward bases in hostile areas, such as Helmand province.

▼ A ground crew unloads a UH-60 Black Hawk from a C-17 Globemaster transport plane in Afghanistan in 2002.

SAFE DELIVERY

Helicopters were vital for moving troops around Afghanistan. The Taliban booby-trapped the roads with explosive devices, so air transportation was much safer than travelling by road.

TALIBAN: An extreme Islamic group that once governed Afghanistan.

GALLERY

Helicopters can be lightning-fast gunships or huge transporters. Their tasks vary from reconnaissance and special forces infiltration to medivac operations and air strikes on enemy targets.

AH-1W SUPER COBRA

First used by American forces in Vietnam, the Super Cobra set the standard for other 'choppers'. It has been in use for over 40 years.

SPECIFICATIONS
Max. load: 6,690 kg
   (14,750 lb)
Crew: 2
Blades: 2 front, 2 tail
Main armament: 20 mm
   cannon

CH-47 CHINOOK

The Chinook dates from 1961. It can carry troops, vital supplies and vehicles – even smaller helicopters.

SPECIFICATIONS
Max. load: 22,680 kg (50,000 lb)
Crew: 3
Blades: 3 front, 3 tail
Main armament: 3 machine
   guns

MEDIVAC: Military shorthand for 'medical evacuation'.

MI-24 HIND

The Russian-built Mi-24 Hind is a combat-assault helicopter and a gunship. The Soviet Union used it in its war in Afghanistan in the 1980s.

SPECIFICATIONS
Max. load: 12,000 kg (26,500 lb)
Crew: 2 or 3
Blades: 5 front, 3 tail
Armament: 12.7 mm machine gun

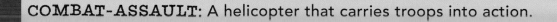

COMBAT-ASSAULT: A helicopter that carries troops into action.

GALLERY

The Eurocopter HAP Tiger is one of the world's most advanced attack helicopters. The pilot and gunner wear helmet-mounted sights. The Tiger's armour can withstand cannon fire.

HAP TIGER

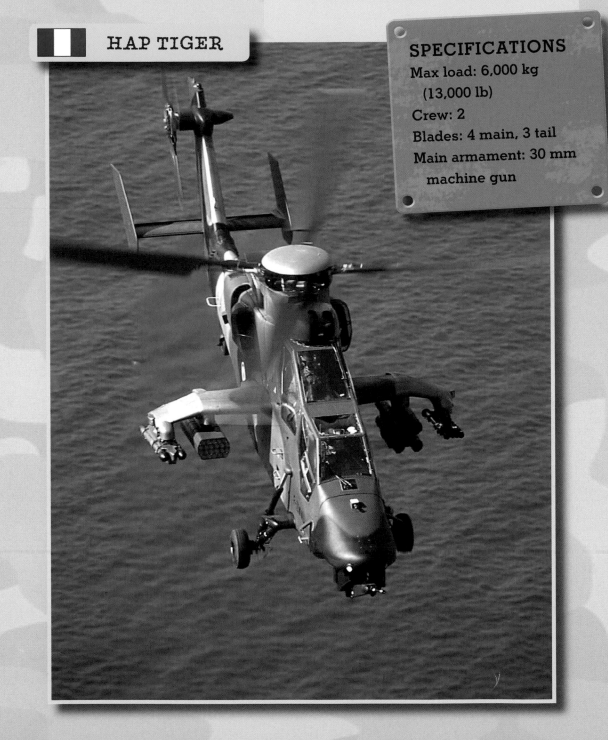

SPECIFICATIONS
Max load: 6,000 kg (13,000 lb)
Crew: 2
Blades: 4 main, 3 tail
Main armament: 30 mm machine gun

HELMET-MOUNTED SIGHTS: Aim at wherever the wearer is looking.

BELL UH–1Y VENOM

SPECIFICATIONS
Max. load: 8,390 kg (18,500 lb)
Crew: 1–4
Blades: 4 main, 2 tail
Main armament: 7.62 mm
or 0.5-calibre machine gun

The Bell UH-1Y Venom, or 'Super Huey', went into production in 2008. It is primarily used by the U.S. Marine Corps.

AH-64 APACHE

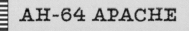

SPECIFICATIONS
Max. load: 10,433 kg (23,000 lb)
Crew: 2
Blades: 4 main, 4 tail
Main armament: Hellfire guided missiles

The AH-64 Apache is the main U.S. Army attack helicopter. It is designed as a fast-response aircraft. It fights best when it is close to the enemy.

GLOSSARY

abseil Term for quickly climbing down a rope.

air drop To deliver supplies from an aircraft, often by parachute.

anti-torque Prevents the rotors spinning the aircraft around.

casevac A military term for casualty evacuation.

combat-assault A helicopter that carries troops into action.

composite A strong material formed by combining other materials.

contours The way a landscape rises and falls.

co-ordination The ability to make different movements at once.

covert Carried out in secret.

deployed Personnel who have been sent out for a particular task.

evacuation Moving someone from danger to safety.

fast-response Ready for action with little warning.

field hospital A temporary hospital set up behind the front line.

fire cover Firing at the enemy to prevent it firing at another target.

gunship A helicopter that carries a powerful range of weapons.

helmet-mounted sights Aims at wherever the wearer is looking.

infantry Troops who are trained to fight on foot.

medivac A military term for medical evacuation.

militia An irregular fighting unit formed by armed civilians.

propellant Fuel that powers an engine to create motion.

reconnaissance Gathering information about enemy activity.

rotorcraft A flying machine powered by a spinning blade or rotor.

sonar buoy A floating device that detects underwater sounds.

storage pod A hard-shelled case carried on a helicopter's wing.

Taliban An extreme Islamic group that once governed Afghanistan.

winch A mechanical drum that winds and unwinds a rope or cable.

FURTHER READING

● BOOKS

Bodden, Valerie. *Helicopters (Built for Battle)*. Creative Paperbacks, 2012.

Bone, Emily. *Helicopters (Usborne Beginners Plus)*. Usborne, 2011.

Colson, Rob Scott. *Ultimate Machines: Helicopters*. Wayland, 2014.

Langley, Andrew. *Helicopters (Machines on the Move)*. Franklin Watts, 2011.

Von Finn, Denny. *HH-60 Pave Hawk Helicopters (Epic Books: Military Vehicles)*. Bellwether Media, 2013.

● WEBSITES

www.ahctv.com/tv-shows/combat-countdown/videos/top-10-helicopters/
Videos of the Top Ten helicopters.

www.airpowerworld.info/helicopters/
Copyright-free images of military helicopters for school assignments.

inventors.about.com/od/militaryhistoryinventions/ss/helicopter_.htm
Profiles of military helicopters with links to pages on helicopter history.

www.guncopter.com/
Directory of helicopter gunships with profiles and photographs.

INDEX